Lazy, Lonely Roley

Jeanne Willis
Illustrated by Joe Boddy

Rigby
A Harcourt Achieve Imprint

www.Rigby.com
1-800-531-5015

Roley was a rhino.
He lived in a zoo.

He was the only rhino.
He had nothing to do.

"Get into the crate!"
the Rhino Keeper said.

But the lazy, lonely rhino
just stayed in his bed.

The Rhino Keeper went
to fetch a giant rope.

Then he tried to pull Roley
up the short slope.

The Bird Keeper came,
and the Bear Keeper, too.

They said, "Pull and we'll push.
That's what we will do."

The distance was short.
The speed was slow.

But into the crate,
Roley would not go.

The Giraffe Keeper came.
He told Roley the plan.

**Then into the crate,
that lazy rhino ran!**

The Rhino Keeper took Roley
to an even bigger zoo.
There were games to play
and lots of things to do.

He was not the only rhino.
He was now one of four.

So Roley was not lazy or lonely any more!